Internet Field Trips

An Online Visit to
NORTH AMERICA

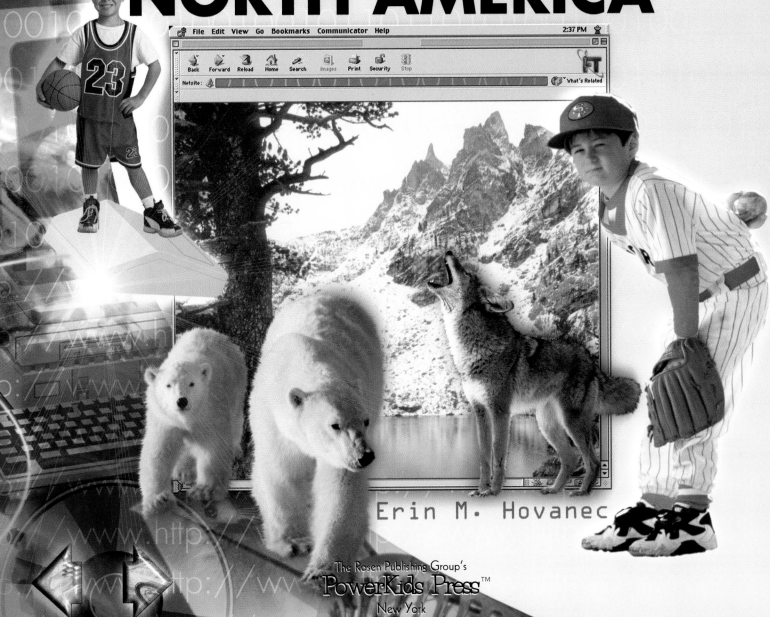

| File Edit View Go Bookmarks Communicator Help | 2:37 PM |

Back Forward Reload Home Search Images Print Security Stop

Netsite:　　　　　　　　　　　　　　　　　　　　　What's Related

Erin M. Hovanec

The Rosen Publishing Group's
PowerKids Press™
New York

For my brother, Joe Hovanec

Published in 2001 by The Rosen Publishing Group, Inc.
29 East 21st Street, New York, NY 10010

First Edition

Book Design: Maria Melendez

Photo Credits: Cover, title page, young baseball player © Bill Tucker/International Stock; title page, polar bears © Tom Murphy/International Stock; title page, Rocky Mountain © Mark Newman/International Stock; title page, raccoon, eagle, and wolf © Digital Stock; p. 7 (Statue of Liberty) © I.T.P./International Stock; p. 8 (Death Valley) © Chuck Szymanski/International Stock; p.11 (Business District of Mexico City) © Sergio Dorantes/CORBIS; p. 12 (Niagara Falls) © Tom Carroll/International Stock; p. 15 (Opossum with babies) © E. R. Degginger/H. Armstrong Roberts; p. 16 (young basketball player dribbling) © Duomo/CORBIS; p. 19 (wafer fabrication) © Lawrence Manning/H. Armstrong Roberts; p. 20 (performers from "CATS") © Nigel Teare/AP Photo.

Hovanec, Erin M.
　　An online visit to North America / Erin M. Hovanec
　　　p. cm.— (Internet field trips)
　　Includes index.
　　Summary: An online trip to various Internet web sites reveals a variety of facts about the continent of North America, the third largest continent on earth.
　　ISBN 0-8239-5654-7
　　1. North America—Computer network resources—Juvenile literature. 2. North America—Computer network resources—Directories—Juvenile literature. 3. Web sites—Directories—Juvenile literature. 4. Children's Web sites—Directories—Juvenile literature. (1. North America.) I. Title II. Series.
　　E38.S.H38 2000　　　　　　　　　　　　　　　　　　　　　　　00-039176
　　025.06'97—dc21

Manufactured in the United States of America

Contents

To Start Surfing....

You may be able to get online without ever leaving home. If you don't have a computer at home, your school or public library will have everything you need to start surfing the Internet. Here's what you'll need:

A personal computer

A personal computer with a monitor, a mouse, and a keyboard.

A modem

A modem is a device that connects your computer to a telephone line and then to other computers.

A telephone connection

A telephone connection, so that your modem can talk to other computers.

Internet software

Internet software programs to tell your computer how to use the Internet.

An Internet Service Provider

An Internet Service Provider. ISP companies allow you to get on the Internet for a small fee every month.

Start Your Engines!

Would you like to explore North America? You can visit the busy streets of New York City, hike through Canadian wilderness, build sandcastles in Mexico, and more, all on the Internet. The Internet is a huge connection of computers called the "World Wide Web," the "Web," or the "Net." You find information on the Internet by using a search engine. Search engines are computer programs that sort through millions of pieces of information. They can help you find lots of free information on the Internet. Type the words "North America" into the search engine, you'll see a list of hyperlinks. These colored words connect one Web page about North America to another.

5

Explore "North America"

North America is the third largest **continent** on Earth. Only Asia and Africa are larger. North America is 9.4 million square miles (24.3 million sq km) in size. It includes Canada, Greenland, the United States, Mexico, Central America, and the Caribbean islands. Together, North America and South America make up Earth's Western **Hemisphere**. The continent of North America is almost completely surrounded by water. The Pacific Ocean lies to the west coast of North America. The Atlantic Ocean lies along its east coast. The Arctic Ocean is to its north. The Caribbean Sea and the Gulf of Mexico separate North America from South America.

6

Some people who visit North America see the Statue of Liberty in New York Harbor. The globe has a map of North America.

To learn more about North America:
http://www.eplay.com/1999-06-19/mapit-zapit/mapitzapit
http://www.nationalgeographic.com/maps/index.html

Back　Forward　Reload　Home　Search　Images　Print　Security　Stop

Netsite:　　　　　　　　　　　　　　　　　　　　　　　　　　What's Related

To learn more about climate:
http://www.ems.psu.edu/WeatherWorld/
http://www.meto.govt.uk/sec3/namerica.html

Every Kind of Climate

North America has just about every type of **climate** on Earth. It has bitter cold and **tropical** heat. It also has wet and dry weather. Most of North America is warm in the summer and cold in the winter. Some parts of the continent, however, have very different climates. For example, much of Greenland is covered with ice, and the temperature rarely reaches above freezing. North America's lowest temperature ever, -87 degrees Fahrenheit (-66° C), was recorded there. The jungles of Central America have hot and very wet weather. Other parts of the continent are hot but very dry. Death Valley, California, is a place with hot, dry weather.

This photo shows Death Valley. North America's highest temperature, 134 degrees Fahrenheit (57° C), was recorded there in 1913.

9

All About Geography

North America has some really interesting **geography**. Two of the four largest countries on Earth, Canada and the United States, are located on the continent. Greenland is the largest island in the world. Twenty-three countries in all make up North America. They include, the Bahamas, Costa Rica, Cuba, and Jamaica. About 300 million people live in North America. Of all the North American countries, the United States has the largest **population**. There are more than 250 million people in the United States. Mexico City, Mexico, is the continent's most populated city, with over 16 million people.

This is a view of Mexico City's business section. This city has the largest population in North America. ▶

To see the geography of North American countries:
http://www.3datlas.com/main_co.html
http://www.atlapedia.com/online/map_index.htm

Back Forward Reload Home Search Images Print Security Stop

Netsite: What's Related

To learn more about North America's natural wonders:
http://www.nationalgeographic.com/media/books/grandcanyon/
index.html
http://www.gorp.com/gorp/location/canada/ontario/algonqui.htm

North American
NATURAL WONDERS

From icy mountains to sunny beaches, from dry deserts to wet rainforests, North America has many beautiful natural places. The Rocky Mountain Range, one of the longest in the world, runs from Alaska into northern Mexico. The continent's tallest mountain is Mount McKinley, in the Alaska Range. This mountain rises to 20,320 feet (6,194 m). Lake Superior, which lies between the United States and Canada, is the world's largest freshwater lake. The colorful rocks and unusual formation of the Grand Canyon make it a great wonder of the world. Niagara Falls and Yosemite Falls attract people from around the globe.

Niagara Falls is part of a boundary line between Canada and the United States. This photo shows the Horseshoe Falls on the Canadian side of the falls.

13

Animals Everywhere!

To see some cool creatures, look no farther than your computer monitor. Animals like beavers, grizzly bears, moose, and opossums all live in North America. You can find coyotes and wolves there, too. Don't get too close, though. Jaguars and leopards walk the jungles of Central America. Polar bears, seals, and whales live in the chilly north, while alligators, monkeys, and parrots make their home in the south.

Crabs, cod, flounder, and lobster are just a few of the creatures that swim in the waters around North America. Many beautiful birds, such as bald eagles, Canadian geese, and snowy owls fly overhead.

14

Opossums are North American animals. When mother opossums move from one place to another, they carry their babies in a pouch.

To see North American animals:
http://www.fpl.com/html/kid_eagle.html
http://www.geocities.com/EnchantedForest/Cottage/8217/
northamericananimals.html

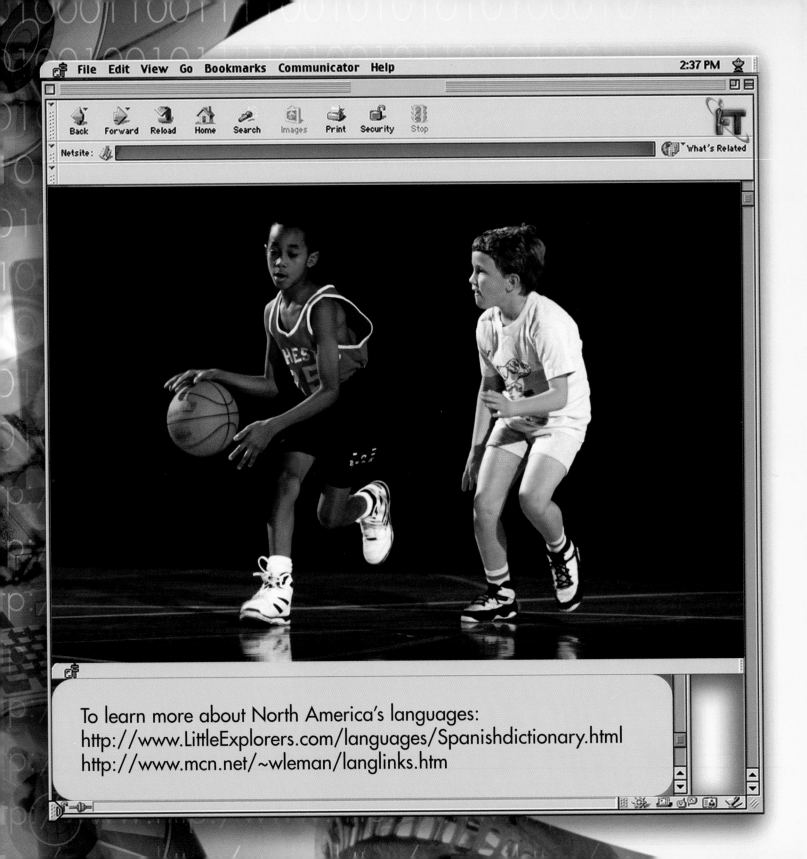

To learn more about North America's languages:
http://www.LittleExplorers.com/languages/Spanishdictionary.html
http://www.mcn.net/~wleman/langlinks.htm

Who Lives in North America?

Thousands of years ago, Native Americans were the first people to live on this continent. Since then people from many different **ethnic groups** have **migrated** to North America. More than half of North America's total population lives in the United States. Most of the people on the continent speak English. However, many Canadians speak French. In Mexico and Central America, most people speak Spanish.

Religion is very important to people in North America. Most people there are Christians. Many others belong to religions, such as Judaism, Islam, Buddhism, or traditional Native American religions.

◀ *People in North America often come from different backgrounds, but they work hard to get along.*

Exciting Industries

People in North America have all kinds of jobs! **Manufacturing**, or making goods, is an important North American **industry**. **Factories** in many countries produce chemicals, clothing, foods, and other items. **Technology** is a fast-growing industry in North America, too, especially in the United States. Many people work with computers and the Internet. In Mexico, Central America, and parts of the United States and Canada, many people work in **agriculture**. They grow crops of grains, fruits, and vegetables. They also raise animals. In Canada and the United States, forestry, or raising trees for wood, is also a major industry.

18

The people in this photo produce computer chips. They dress in special clothing to make sure they don't ▶ harm their products with dust or dirt.

To learn about technology and industry in North America:
http://www.pbs.org/wgbh/amex/kids/index.html
http://www.odci.gov/cia/publications/factbook

To learn more about North American art and music:
http://www.nmaa.si.edu/
http://www.tigtail.org/TVM/B/Bfp.html

North American Art

The first North American artists were the Native Americans. They created beautiful clothing, jewelry, and everyday objects like bowls and vases. Since then, North America has produced forms of entertainment that people around the world enjoy. New York City's Broadway plays and musical shows are great attractions. For many years, Hollywood, California, has been the movie capital of the world. North American musicians produce a wide range of music. They create and perform spirituals, blues, jazz, bluegrass, Louisiana Cajun music, Caribbean calypso, country and western, Mexican mariachi, rock and roll, salsa, and hip-hop.

◀ The show "Cats" ran on Broadway for 18 years and had 7,485 performances. It became the longest running show in the history of Broadway.

Don't Stop Searching Now!

You'll never run out of fun facts to learn about North America. It is such a big continent. It's filled with different peoples and places. From the giant redwoods of California to the palm trees of Central America, from the rocky shores of Canada to the white sands of Bermuda, you'll never run out of things to do in North America. Every North American country is unique, and every state in the United States is different. Here are two terrific Web sites about this continent:
http://www.enchantedlearning.com/school/USA/
http://www.ZoomSchool.com/school/Canada/
Where's your favorite place in North America?

G L O S S A R Y

agriculture (A-grih-kul-cher) Farming and raising animals.

climate (KLY-mit) The type of weather that a certain area has.

continent (KON-tin-ent) One of the seven great masses of land on Earth.

ethnic groups (ETH-nik GROOPS) Groups of people having the same race, culture, language, or belonging to the same country.

factories (FAK-tuh-reez) Places where goods are made.

geography (jee-AH-gruh-fee) The study of the features of Earth's surface, climate, continents, countries, and people.

hemisphere (HEH-muh-sfeer) A half of Earth's surface.

industry (IN-des-tree) A business that makes a product or provides a service.

manufacturing (man-yoo-FAK-cher-ing) Making something by hand or with a machine, usually in large amounts.

migrated (MY-gray-ted) When large groups of people or animals have moved from one place to another.

population (pop-yoo-LAY-shun) The number of people who live in a region.

technology (tek-NAL-uh-jee) Industry that deals with electronics and computers.

tropical (TRAH-pih-kul) An area that is very hot and humid.

Index

Web Sites

Check out the exciting Web sites about North America on these pages: pp. 7, 8, 11, 12, 15, 16, 19, 20, and 22.